30 DAYS
to
Pray

AND ALIGN YOUR HEART WITH GOD

DEVOTIONAL JOURNAL

JASON NICHOLAS BAILEY

30 Days to Pray and Align Your Heart with God

© 2025 Jason Nicholas Bailey

Published by Zophos Media

Printed in the United States of America

First Printing 2025

Scripture quotations are from the ESV® Bible (The Holy Bible, English Standard Version®), copyright © 2001 by Crossway, a publishing ministry of Good News Publishers. Used by permission. All rights reserved. Unless otherwise noted, all Scripture quotations are from the ESV® Bible.

Paperback edition ISBN: 979-8-9998844-0-4

Library of Congress Cataloging-in-Publication Data

Bailey, Jason Nicholas.

30 Days to Pray and Align Your Heart with God : devotional journal / Jason Nicholas Bailey. — First edition.

p. cm.

Includes bibliographical references.

ISBN 979-8-9998844-0-4 (pbk.)

1. Prayer—Christian life. 2. Christian life—Biblical teaching. 3. Devotional calendars. 4. Bible—Study and teaching. I. Title.

BV210.3.B35 2025

242—dc23

Library of Congress Control Number: 2025917828

for Paul Giesbrecht

When you asked us to meet at the church every week at 3 a.m. just to pray, we honestly thought you were crazy. But you were serious—and through your example, you taught four young men how to come before the Lord in prayer.

I'll see you again someday.

Author's Note

In the spring of 2025, I began teaching a nine-week series on prayer in a small classroom at our church. That first week, I wasn't sure if anyone would even come—but they did. And week after week, they returned, eager to learn. The room soon became a place of honest questions, thoughtful conversations, and a shared longing to understand prayer more deeply.

I watched people begin to see prayer in a new way—not just as a list of needs, but as a way of drawing closer to God, aligning with His heart, and living with purpose. By the end of the class, several asked if I could share the material so they could keep going. That's what planted the idea for this book.

What you're holding is a reshaped version of those original lessons—written with the same heart and the same hope: that it stirs something in you. I kept it short on purpose, because I want you to think, reflect, and pray as you go.

My prayer is that this helps you grow—not just in what you know about prayer, but in how you live it. That your prayers would become more honest, more consistent, more shaped by Scripture, and ultimately, more transformative.

Thank you for your desire to pray. I believe God honors those who earnestly seek Him.

Contents

Prayers of Petition and Fasting

Prayers of Intercession

Spiritual Warfare and Praying with Authority

Listening in Prayer: Hearing God's Voice

Developing A Consistent Prayer Life

Introduction

For many Christians, prayer has become little more than a place for requests—like submitting a list to a divine vending machine and hoping something good drops out. But if that's all prayer becomes, we're missing the fullness of what God designed it to be.

Prayer is also more than asking for blessings. It is meant to realign us with God's purposes. In short, prayer is where transformation begins.

This short book was written out of my own desire to help believers grow beyond "God, help me," and into "God, make me more like You." What you'll read here is a collection of 30 lessons designed to walk through different aspects of a faithful prayer life.

Each lesson is rooted in Scripture, built around a distinct focus, and guided by a foundational truth: prayer is more about alignment with God than simply getting answers. It's about learning to listen, to worship, to intercede, to confess, and to surrender. It's about becoming someone who isn't just occasionally prayerful, but someone whose life is continually shaped by prayer.

How quickly you move through the content is up to you—but I encourage you to go slowly. Don't rush. Take time each day to engage with a small portion of the material, but spend most of your time reflecting on the lesson and, most importantly, in prayer.

This isn't just a book to read—it's an invitation to pray. Throughout these lessons, you'll find sections for prayer notes. Use them to pause, listen for what the Lord might be saying, and write it down in the space provided. I've included suggested prayers along the way, but don't feel limited by them. Pray in your own words, in your own way, as the Spirit leads.

The goal is not to complete pages, but to learn how to pray—and how to align your heart with God. If you can't do one lesson a day, do one every other day, or one a week. The most important thing is not to give up or let this sit on the shelf.

I want you to see that prayer is not reserved for the super-spiritual or the perfectly behaved—but for ordinary people who are willing to come humbly, boldly, and often.

Most importantly, I want you to see that God desires you to have an active part in advancing His Kingdom. That's the foundation Jesus laid when He taught us to pray, "Your Kingdom come, Your will be done." It's a prayer that doesn't begin with our needs, but with God's purposes. And as we begin to pray like that, our needs and desires begin to take their rightful place under His reign.

That's my hope for you.

That you would be transformed by the renewing of your mind, so that you may discern God's will—His good, pleasing, and perfect will. That you would pray faithfully. That you would pray according to God's Word. And that, through prayer, your life would increasingly reflect the Kingdom you were made for.

One last thing—you'll need a Bible. All scripture references in this book are from the ESV (English Standard Version). If you don't have a Bible, you can download a Bible app on your phone and follow along that way.

Let's begin!

Praying with a Kingdom Mindset

Prayer is more than bringing our needs before God—it's an invitation to align our hearts with His greater purpose. In the next few lessons, we'll explore how Jesus and others modeled a Kingdom-centered approach to prayer, one that shifts the focus away from personal agendas and toward God's will. When we seek His Kingdom first, prayer shifts from presenting our plans to a desire to participate in His eternal purposes.

From Personal Agendas to Kingdom Alignment

Read Matthew 6:10 and Matthew 13:44-46.

The mention of the Kingdom of Heaven in Jesus's prayer shows his focus on the big picture of God's plan. His parable about the Kingdom in Matthew 13 helps us understand the value and majesty of the Kingdom.

Often when we pray, we are not praying with a Kingdom mindset. We only think of the here and now, and our immediate needs. When we pray, we ought to seek alignment with His Kingdom and His mission. When we seek alignment with God's Kingdom, prayer becomes less about the now and more about the future and participation in God's redemptive work.

Read Luke 22:42.

Too often, our prayers are shaped primarily by physical needs—illness, provision, crisis. These are real and important, but they're not the center of Kingdom-minded prayer.

This week, start each prayer by asking:

"Father, what is Your will in this situation? How can I focus on your Kingdom today?

With Kingdom-minded prayer, we can express our desires, but we shift our focus from our own needs to God's eternal plan. It invites us to participate in something far greater than ourselves. When we pray like Jesus—seeking God's will above our own—we begin to see every situation as an opportunity to align with His redemptive work in the world.

Start to view your life through the lens of God's purposes—not just what you want, but what He wants through you for the sake of His Kingdom. Jesus trusted the Father's will as better, and so should we.

Suggested Prayer:

Father,

Teach me to pray with a heart aligned with your will and Your Kingdom. Help me to seek not just my own desires, but Your will, Your glory, and Your purposes. Let my prayers reflect the values of heaven, not the values of earth. May Your Kingdom come, and Your will be done on earth as it is in heaven.

In Jesus' name,

Amen.

Question:

When you come before God in prayer, are you typically in a hurry? Is your mind continually distracted? What can you do to focus more on God this week?

Reflections:

_____

_____

_____

_____

_____

_____

Lesson 2

A Heavenly Country

Read Hebrews 11:1-40.

In the previous lesson, we learned how Jesus taught us to pray, "Thy Kingdom come, thy will be done on earth as it is in heaven" (Matthew 6:10). This mindset—seeking God's Kingdom first—should shape the way we pray.

Hebrews 11 describes faithful men and women who lived with their eyes fixed on something greater than the world around them. Though they didn't receive the fulfillment of every promise in their lifetime, they trusted that God was preparing "a better country—that is, a heavenly one."

We live in a world that runs on instant gratification, where value is often placed on what can be seen, achieved, or experienced right now. But the hope of those described in Hebrews wasn't grounded in immediate answers. It was anchored in the certainty of God's eternal Kingdom. Their prayers and their lives pointed forward to something far greater than earthly success or comfort. In the same way, our prayers should not be limited to asking for quick solutions to present needs. They should align with the reality of what God is building—a Kingdom that cannot be shaken, and a future that far surpasses anything this world offers.

Challenge

When you pray, ask yourself: Am I praying with my eyes fixed on eternity or only on immediate circumstances? Am I seeking God's greater purposes, or am I mainly focused on temporary needs?

Consider whether your actions reflect alignment with the here and now, or with the eternal Kingdom God is building.

If someone were writing a chapter of faith about you, how might it read?

By faith, (your name) did _____.

Suggested Prayer:

Father,

Help me to pray with my eyes fixed on eternity. May I live with trust that goes beyond what I see—believing Your promises even when they feel far off. Give me faith that endures, and a heart that seeks Your greater purpose in all things.

In Jesus' name,

Amen.

Question:

What is one thing you can do this week that you believe God is calling you to do? Would you be content if you didn't see immediate results? Why or why not?

Reflections:

_____

_____

_____

_____

_____

Lesson 3

Elijah and a Kingdom Mindset

Read 1 Kings 18:20–39.

At a time when Israel's heart had grown cold and divided, Elijah stood alone as God's prophet against hundreds of false prophets and a nation steeped in idolatry. The scene is tense and public. Elijah calls out the people for trying to serve both Baal and the Lord.

As the prophets of Baal cry out with frantic energy—shouting, dancing, even cutting themselves—Elijah watches and waits. Their prayers are full of noise but empty of power. In contrast, Elijah rebuilds the altar of the Lord (v. 30), symbolically restoring true worship before offering his prayer. He drenches the sacrifice in water, making it humanly impossible for fire to consume it—then prays simply, confidently, and clearly.

God answers with undeniable power—fire falls from heaven and consumes the sacrifice, the water, the stones, and even the dust (v. 38). There's no question: He alone is the true and living God.

Look closely at Elijah's prayer. He isn't performing for attention—he's doing three things (v. 36-37):

1. He's done all these things by instruction from God.

2. He wants the people to recognize who God truly is.

3. He trusts that God is already at work turning their hearts back to Himself.

Elijah didn't manufacture a moment. He simply aligned himself with what God had already planned. This is Kingdom alignment! The miracle happened because God willed it—not because Elijah had special power.

When God moves, it is always to reveal Himself and draw people back to Him. Elijah understood both God's purpose and his own role in fulfilling it. We'll come back to Elijah later, but for now, focus on why he was able to do the things he did. It wasn't about Elijah's power—it was about his alignment with the will of God.

Suggested Prayer:

Father,

Make me bold like Elijah—not for my own glory, but so others may see You clearly. Help me stand firm in faith, trusting Your power and not my own. Align my heart with Yours, so that my prayers reflect Your purpose.

In Jesus' name,

Amen.

Question:

Do you also desire for people to know God? Do you trust that God could use you to help turn someone's heart back to Him?

Reflections:

_____

_____

_____

_____

_____

_____

Praying with Faith

In the previous three lessons, we explored how Jesus taught us to pray with a heart aligned to God's Kingdom and will. We continue building on that foundation by turning to the kind of faith that supports true, Kingdom-centered prayer—a faith that believes God is present, hears us, and responds to those who seek Him. The examples of faithful men and women in Scripture remind us that prayer is not just about speaking words, but about coming to God with a deep trust in who He is and what He has promised. Even when the outcome is unseen, this kind of prayer invites us to trust, to wait, and to surrender—believing that what God is building is far greater than what we can see right now.

"And without faith it is impossible to please God, because anyone who comes to him must believe that he exists and that he rewards those who earnestly seek him" (Hebrews 11:6).

Faith changes everything about how we pray. It draws us into a deep trust—knowing that God is present, that He hears us, and that He is already at work.

Lesson 4

Faith Behind Prayer

The strength of our faith should not rest on how many prayers we've seen answered—it must be anchored in who God is and what He has promised. If our confidence in God rises and falls based on outcomes, then we've built our faith on circumstances, not on His unchanging character.

True faith moves us to act—not because we see the outcome, but because we trust that God is already at work, accomplishing His eternal purposes even when we can't see it (Hebrews 11:1).

Read Hebrews 11:8 and Acts 8:26-27.

Abraham was called to leave everything familiar and go to a land God would show him—without a map, a timeline, or a guarantee of what lay ahead. He obeyed, simply because God said to go.

Centuries later, Philip received a similar instruction from the Holy Spirit: "Go toward the south to the road that goes down from Jerusalem to Gaza" (Acts 8:26). He had no idea why. But he went. And on that road, he met an Ethiopian official whose life would be forever changed through the gospel.

In both cases, the call was clear—even if the outcome wasn't. Their faith was demonstrated in obedience, not in foresight.

Read Matthew 8:8-10.

When a Roman centurion came to Jesus on behalf of his sick servant, he made a remarkable statement of faith:

"Lord, I am not worthy to have You come under my roof, but only say the word, and my servant will be healed."

Jesus marveled at his faith. This kind of trust didn't demand signs or proof. It simply recognized the power and authority of the One being asked.

As you continue to pray, ask God to deepen your faith—not just for answered requests, but for trust in who He is.

Suggested Prayer:

Father,

Help me to pray with the kind of faith that trusts You even when I don't see the whole path. Like Abraham, Philip, and the centurion, teach me to believe in Your power, Your promises, and Your goodness—no matter what I feel or understand. Anchor my faith in who You are, not just in what I see.

In Jesus' name,

Amen.

Question:

Do you have a hard time trusting God? Take some time, and think through why this might be and how you can increase your faith.

Reflections:

_____

_____

_____

_____

_____

_____

Lesson 5

Faithful Among Lions

Read Daniel 6:1-23.

When a law was passed forbidding prayer to anyone but the king, Daniel "got down on his knees three times a day and prayed and gave thanks before his God, as he had done previously" (Daniel 6:10).

Daniel remained faithful to God, knowing the cost. He didn't compromise or wait for things to calm down. His faith in God's sovereignty outweighed any fear of man-made decrees.

King Darius, though distressed, said to Daniel, "May your God, whom you serve continually, deliver you!" (Daniel 6:16). Even the king could see that Daniel's faith was unshakable.

Later, Daniel testified: "My God sent his angel and shut the lions' mouths, and they have not harmed me, because I was found blameless before him" (Daniel 6:22). Verse 23 adds, "No kind of harm was found on him, because he had trusted in his God."

Daniel's story is a powerful reminder that a consistent prayer life isn't just a spiritual habit—it's an anchor in the storm. His unwavering trust in God was evident not only in his words but in his willingness to risk everything rather than break that communion. In the face of danger, Daniel didn't panic—he prayed. And God, faithful as ever, honored that trust with protection and deliverance. More than anything, this moment reveals how real Daniel's relationship with God truly was. Imagine being told you could no longer speak to someone you deeply love—and instead, were required to talk to someone else. You'd refuse. That's what Daniel did. As you continue through this book, ask God to deepen your love for Him—to give you the kind of faith that endures even in the hardest of times, and to help you continue to pray even when you're surrounded by lions.

Suggested Prayer:

Father,

Like Daniel, help me stay faithful to You no matter the cost. Teach me to seek You not just when things go wrong, but every day. Help me love You more, and give me the courage to trust You above all else. Let my life be a testimony to others, just like Daniel's.

In Jesus' name,

Amen.

Question:

Do you only pray when you need something? What would it take for you to pray as consistently as Daniel did?

Reflections:

_____

_____

_____

_____

_____

_____

Lesson 6

Turning to God in Faith and Humility

Read 1 Samuel 1:1–20.

In her anguish, Hannah turned to God for what seemed impossible. Her prayer was whispered—perhaps barely audible—but it was full of faith. Hannah believed so deeply that she promised to dedicate her one and only son fully to God's service—a beautiful foreshadowing of Christ.

Read Luke 18:9–14.

How was the faith and prayer of the tax collector similar to the faith and prayer of Hannah? Was his prayer focused on boasting about his actions, or on his need for forgiveness and a right relationship with God?

Read Matthew 6:7–8.

What matters more in prayer—many words, or a sincere heart?

Just like Hannah and the tax collector, we're invited to come to God with honest hearts, not polished performances. God already knows what we need—but He wants us to trust Him enough to bring those needs before Him. Prayer isn't about getting the words right; it's about having real faith.

The people described in Hebrews 11 weren't chasing quick answers or short-term relief. They prayed and lived with eternity in mind, believing God was doing something greater—even when they couldn't yet see it. That same invitation stands for us.

If you've ever felt unsure about how to pray, remember: what matters most isn't the length or eloquence of your prayer, but the sincerity behind it. Faith doesn't mean never struggling—it means returning to God anyway. Even if your only words are, "Lord, I believe—help my unbelief," that's enough. God honors that kind of faith—faith that leans forward into His promises, even while patiently waiting.

Suggested Prayer:

Father,

Help me to come to You with a sincere heart—honest, humble, and full of faith. Teach me to trust You even when I'm waiting, even when I don't have the words. Remind me that You see my heart and hear even my whispers. Help me to trust in who You are, not just focus on what I want or need.

In Jesus' name,

Amen.

Question:

How do you approach God in prayer? Do you believe God hears you? What do these passages prove?

Reflections:

_____

_____

_____

_____

_____

_____

Prayers of Thanksgiving and Worship

Prayer isn't just about asking—it's also about adoring. When we pause to fix our eyes on who God is and what He has done, our hearts are lifted, and our perspective begins to shift. David understood this well. In Psalm 34:1–6, we see his determination to praise God not after his fears had passed, but right in the midst of them—"at all times." His worship was rooted in God's character, not in his circumstances. David rejoiced in knowing God, and he invited others to join him: "Let us exalt his name together." In this section, we will focus on offering prayers of thanksgiving and worship.

A Heart of Gratitude

"Make a joyful noise to the Lord, all the earth! Serve the Lord with gladness! Come into His presence with singing! Know that the Lord, He is God! It is He who made us, and we are His; we are His people, and the sheep of His pasture (Psalm 100)."

In its original context, the "we" in "we are His people" referred to Israel. But notice how the psalm opens: "all the earth." From the very beginning, it's a universal call to worship—an invitation for the whole world to praise God.

It starts with a call to make a joyful noise—that's not silent prayer. That's an audible sound of praise. You don't have to be quiet when you pray, and if you sing, you definitely don't have to be a great singer. What matters is the heart behind it. When you pray, worship God for who He is.

Psalm 100 also says to serve the Lord with gladness. That means even in our actions and obedience, there should be joy. Serving God isn't just about doing the right things—it's about doing them with a heart that delights in Him. When you understand who God is, what He has done, and what He's still doing in your life, joy and thankfulness naturally rise up from within.

Have you ever been so grateful for something someone did that words didn't feel like enough? You wanted to respond—not just with thanks, but with action. That's what a heart of gratitude toward God looks like. It's not just expressed with words but with a desire to respond, to give, to serve, to worship. In other words, prayer and worship is just the beginning.

Pay attention to the action words in this passage: make, serve, come, and know. Everything flows from that last one—knowing God. It's the foundation for joyful worship and glad-hearted service. It's what gives you the desire to come into His presence with singing. As you read God's Word, ask Him to reveal more of who He is and how deeply He loves you.

If you're not sure what to be thankful for, start here: thank Him for giving you life.

Suggested Prayer:

Father,

Let my prayers not only be about my needs and the needs of others, but also be filled with thanksgiving and gratitude for who You are and what You've done. May You increase my faith, and may my faith lead to action.

In Jesus' name,

Amen.

Question:

Is it hard for you to pray prayers of thanksgiving and have a heart of gratitude? Why or why not?

Reflections:

_____

_____

_____

_____

_____

_____

Lesson 8

David's Pattern of Praise

Read 1 Chronicles 29:10-13, 2 Samuel 7:18-29, and Psalm 103.

In 1 Chronicles 29, count how many times you see the words "you" and "yours." Now count how many times you read "my" or "mine." Praising God begins with shifting the focus from ourselves to God.

We talked about thankfulness in the last lesson. Notice how thanksgiving comes after proclaiming who God is and what He has done.

When you read these passages, you'll notice something steady in the way David prays. Whether he's celebrating a victory or sitting in awe of God's promises, his heart posture doesn't change—he starts with worship. He remembers who God is, not just what God has done. You see humility in the way he views himself before God, and you hear genuine thankfulness in his words.

David doesn't treat prayer like a transaction. He doesn't rush in asking for things. Instead, he begins by declaring God's greatness and then reflects on how personally involved God is in his life. That combination—God's power and God's care—shapes the way David prays.

The challenge for us is to pray like that. Not just when things are good, but especially when they're not. David's prayers remind us that worship isn't something we add on to prayer—it's where prayer begins. And worship begins with knowing God and shifting our focus to Him: His purposes, His power, and His Kingdom.

This week, as you continue to pray, try to balance how much you talk about your needs with how much you proclaim and praise God. Take note if there's an imbalance and ask yourself why. You may find that you're more focused on what you want to be done than on what God wants to do in and through your life.

Pause, reflect, and consider David's pattern of praise.

Suggested Prayer:

Father,

Like David, help me come before You with a heart of praise and worship. Teach me to remember Your faithfulness in every season—your mercy, love, and promises that never fail. Remind me to fill my prayers with awe and gratitude, remembering that all I have comes from You.

In Jesus' name,

Amen.

Question:

Do your prayers currently focus more on you or God? How can your prayers begin to reflect David's pattern of praise?

Reflections:

_____

_____

_____

_____

_____

_____

Lesson 9

Worship Reshapes Our Perspective

Read Psalm 145:1-21.

As we continue to think about worship through prayer, this passage reminds us that worship isn't just something we feel—it's something we choose. It's intentional. David doesn't wait for the perfect moment or a certain mood. He says, "I will extol you... I will bless you... every day I will praise you." These are decisions. And the words he uses—extol, bless, praise, commend, declare—are all active. Worship, for David, is something he does on purpose.

David also understands that praise is not a private act. It's contagious. "One generation shall commend your works to another," he writes. In other words, our worship today shapes the faith of those who come after us. He also says, "The eyes of all look to you," and "The Lord is near to all who call on him in truth." The invitation is wide open—no one is left out who looks to the Lord. "He fulfills the desire of those who fear him... he hears their cry and saves them." God is not distant or disinterested. He is actively preserving those who love Him.

But David also draws a sharp contrast: "The Lord preserves all who love him, but all the wicked he will destroy." Part of worship is acknowledging God's justice. We praise Him not just for His kindness and compassion, but also for His righteousness and His authority to judge evil. A God who never judged would not be worthy of reverence. True worship involves both awe and alignment—praising God not only for what He gives, but for who He is.

David ends the psalm with a final personal resolve: "My mouth will speak the praise of the Lord, and let all flesh bless his holy name forever and ever." It echoes the strong declaration found in Joshua 24:15: "But as for me and my house, we will serve the Lord." Both men stood in a moment of clarity, drawing a line and choosing whom they would honor—not just occasionally, but every day.

Suggested Prayer:

Father,

Teach me to worship You not just when I feel like it, but as a daily choice. Help me to praise You on purpose—to declare Your greatness with my words and my life. Let my worship overflow even in the middle of challenges.

In Jesus' name,

Amen.

Question:

In this lesson, we see that David makes a deliberate choice to worship God, using phrases like "I will…" What can you learn from his example about choosing to worship—even when you don't feel like it?

Reflections:

_____

_____

_____

_____

_____

_____

Lesson 10

Beyond the Amen

Read Hebrews 13:15–16 and Colossians 3:16–17.

We're called to offer a continual sacrifice of praise—the fruit of lips that acknowledge God's name. But Hebrews adds something else: Do not neglect to do good and to share what you have, for such sacrifices are pleasing to God. In other words, prayer doesn't stop at what we say. It shows up in what we do. Prayer leads to participation. A life that honors God is marked by both gratitude and generosity.

Prayer should lead us to act. Not out of guilt or pressure, but because we've been with God—and we can't stay the same. We begin to live with thankfulness instead of complaint. We look for ways to serve instead of waiting to be served. We find ourselves offering praise not only with our lips, but with our time, our resources, and our attention. That's the kind of worship God desires—not perfection, but a willing heart.

Colossians 3 points in the same direction. "Let the word of Christ dwell in you richly," Paul writes. That's more than reading a verse in the morning or saying a quick prayer at night. It's about allowing God's truth to take root—to settle deep into us until it shapes what we teach, how we encourage, what we sing, and how we live. Paul's conclusion is simple but weighty: whatever you do, in word or deed, do everything in the name of the Lord Jesus, giving thanks. Worship, then, becomes a way of life. It's found in our routines, in our decisions, in our relationships. It's in the way we carry ourselves when no one's watching, and in how we respond when others are in need.

So don't let prayer stop at the amen. Let it move you. Let it carry over into how you live, how you give, and how you love. Let the word of Christ dwell in you so richly that your life becomes a mirror, reflecting the heart of God to the people around you.

Suggested Prayer:

Father,

Help me to act not out of duty, but out of a genuine desire to join You in the work You are doing. Let my actions become an expression of worship. May I not only pray for others, but also serve them as You would.

In Jesus' name,

Amen.

Question:

How can you go beyond the "amen" this week and serve the person you've prayed for in a real, tangible way?

Reflections:

_____

_____

_____

_____

_____

Prayers of Confession and Repentance

Now we turn to a vital part of our prayer life that often feels difficult but is important for our relationship with God—confession and repentance.

The prophet Daniel models this for us:

"I prayed to the Lord my God and confessed:

'Lord, the great and awesome God, who keeps his covenant of love with those who love him and keep his commandments, we have sinned and done wrong. We have been wicked and have rebelled; we have turned away from your commands and laws" (Daniel 9:4-5).

Confession is not simply admitting wrongs—it is an honest reckoning with our sin and repentance is an intentional turning back to God's heart. Ask God to show you areas of your life that you need to surrender to Him.

Lesson 11

Honest with God, Honest with Ourselves

David's words in Psalm 32 reveal the burden of unconfessed sin: "When I kept silent, my bones wasted away" (Psalm 32:3).

Sin can weigh us down deeply—not just spiritually but emotionally and even physically. It steals joy, peace, and separates us from God. When David chose honesty and confession, he found relief and freedom:

"I acknowledged my sin to you, and I did not cover my iniquity; I said, 'I will confess my transgressions to the Lord,' and you forgave the guilt of my sin" (Psalm 32:5).

Confession isn't about telling God something He doesn't already know. God is all-knowing and sees everything. Rather, confession is about aligning ourselves with the truth—being honest with God and with ourselves.

John writes plainly:

"If we say we have no sin, we deceive ourselves, and the truth is not in us. If we confess our sins, he is faithful and just to forgive us our sins and to cleanse us from all unrighteousness" (1 John 1:8-9).

When we ignore or hide our sin, it creates distance between us and God. Isaiah 59:1-2 clearly states, "Your iniquities have separated you from your God; your sins have hidden his face from you..." Sin breaks fellowship with God and disrupts the closeness we're meant to have with Him.

God doesn't ask you to clean yourself up first—He simply asks you to come honestly. Confession is the doorway to grace, and salvation begins with admitting your need for Him. Jesus came not for the perfect, but for the broken—for those willing to turn from sin and trust in Him. If you're feeling the weight of guilt or the pull of conviction, it's an invitation to be honest with yourself and with God, who knows you better than anyone.

Suggested Prayer:

Father,

Today, I come to You honestly. I confess my faults, my failures, and the ways I've turned from You. Thank You that You are faithful and just to forgive. Remove my pride.

In Jesus' name,

Amen.

Question:

Do you have anyone in your life who can help hold you accountable for things you are struggling with? Consider reaching out to them this week.

Reflections:

_____

_____

_____

_____

_____

_____

A Broken and Contrite Heart

After confession, when the truth is no longer hidden, there comes a sobering moment—a reckoning that humbles the soul. This is not about self-pity or shame, but a spiritual brokenness that clears away pride and softens the heart before God. It is the ground where healing begins.

Psalm 51 gives us a powerful picture of this through David's prayer after his sin with Bathsheba was exposed. Faced with the gravity of what he had done (2 Samuel 11-12), David didn't shift blame or retreat into denial. He brought his shattered heart to God:

"Create in me a clean heart, O God, and renew a right spirit within me... The sacrifices of God are a broken spirit; a broken and contrite heart, O God, you will not despise" (Psalm 51:10, 17).

In this moment, David wasn't just confessing—he was laid bare, fully aware of his own frailty, yet turning to the only One who could restore him.

David's prayer isn't about reclaiming comfort or status. He longs for restoration with God—asking for a clean heart, a renewed spirit, and God's presence to remain with him. This shows us that God desires sincerity and humility above all. A broken and contrite heart is never rejected by Him.

But repentance doesn't end with the heart—it overflows into the way we live. John the Baptist called people to

"Bear fruit in keeping with repentance" (Matthew 3:8),

and Peter reminded us to

"Repent, then, and turn to God, so that your sins may be wiped out, that times of refreshing may come from the Lord" (Acts 3:19-20).

As you pray, invite God to search your heart. Be honest about where you've fallen short, and ask Him to do the renewing work only He can do. But don't stop there—ask Him to give you strength to live out this repentance, bearing fruit that reflects the change in your heart.

> *"Create in me a clean heart, O God, and renew a right spirit within me... The sacrifices of God are a broken spirit; a broken and contrite heart, O God, you will not despise."*
>
> **Psalm 51:10, 17**

Unlike the earlier lessons, this one doesn't include a suggested prayer. Only you know what you struggle with. I invite you to take a few moments to pray in your own words—slowly and honestly—confessing your sins to Him. Ask God to reveal any unconfessed sin or ongoing struggle, and pray that your confession and desire for restoration will lead to repentance and a deeper walk with Him.

The Kindness That Leads to Repentance

Repentance follows confession and brokenness. Turning our hearts back to God is when true change starts. But repentance is more than just saying "I'm sorry." It's a deliberate turning away from sin and a turning toward God's loving heart.

Romans 2:4 reminds us:

"Or do you presume on the riches of his kindness and forbearance and patience, not knowing that God's kindness is meant to lead you to repentance?"

God's kindness is not an excuse to continue living a life of sin. Rather, it's intended to lead you to repentance—so you can turn from your sin, return to where you belong, and be welcomed with open arms.

Read Luke 15:11-24.

This truth shines clearly in Jesus' story of the prodigal son. After squandering his inheritance, the son prepares a speech to try to earn his place back. But before he can say a word, his father sees him from a distance, runs to him, and embraces him. There's no condemnation, no delay—only welcome and love.

That's how God responds when we repent and turn back to Him—He's been waiting all along, ready to restore the relationship.

Maybe your experience with your earthly father makes this kind of love hard to imagine. That's okay—you're not alone. But this is who God is: a Father who meets you right where you are, with all your faults, pain, and baggage.

If you've walked away from God, it's time to come home. You might feel like you can't—that He wouldn't accept you. But that's not true. Come to your Father in prayer. That's the first step toward home.

Suggested Prayer:

Father,

Thank You for Your kindness that gently draws me back when I wander. Help me to see repentance not as a burden, but as a loving turn toward You—a chance to be restored and embraced just like the prodigal son. Jesus, remove shame and fear, and fill me with the joy of Your forgiveness.

In Jesus' name,

Amen.

Question:

Is the Lord gently drawing you to repent of a sin or struggle in your life? Are you ready to pray about it?

Reflections:

_____

_____

_____

_____

_____

Prayers of Petition and Fasting

We've seen how prayer rooted in a Kingdom mindset transforms us and how faith, worship, confession, and repentance deepen our relationship with God. This section, we focus on petition—the part of prayer where we bring our requests boldly before God—and the powerful discipline of fasting that often accompanies earnest asking.

God invites us to ask—not timidly or hesitantly, but boldly and persistently. Jesus not only gives us permission to bring our needs before God, He also teaches us how to do it well.

A Petition That Begins with Trust

Read Matthew 7:7-11 and 1 John 5:14-15.

Matthew 7 is often quoted for the promise of asking and receiving, but it's important to see this teaching in the broader context of the chapter. Jesus isn't offering a simple formula for getting what we want. The chapter includes warnings about judgment, calls for obedience, and the need to build our lives on solid ground. The invitation to ask, seek, and knock (Matthew 7:7-11) fits within this larger call to authentic faith—one that trusts God as a loving Father who gives good gifts, and that follows Him with a surrendered heart.

This means that petition isn't a demand placed on God, but a sign of a relationship. It's bold, yet humble—rooted in reverence and trust. 1 John 5:14-15 makes this clear: "If we ask anything according to his will, he hears us. And if we know that he hears us—whatever we ask—we know that we have what we asked of him." Our prayers are heard when they align with God's will.

When we come to God in prayer, asking boldly, we also come ready to listen and obey. God's answers reflect His perfect wisdom, timing, and goodness, which are often revealed as we seek Him earnestly. So the promise of ask, seek, knock is not about entitlement—it's about trust.

Petition begins with trust—trusting that God hears us and responds in ways that shape us, grow us, and ultimately work for the good of those who love Him and are called according to His purpose (Romans 8:28).

But what does it actually look like to bring our requests before God with that kind of trust?

We see it clearly in Jesus' prayer in Gethsemane:

"Father, if you are willing, take this cup from me; yet not my will, but yours be done" (Luke 22:42).

In this moment, Jesus is expressing His human desire honestly while fully submitting to God's plan. As both fully God and fully man, Jesus shows us what perfect trust looks like. His divine will is united with the Father's, but in His humanity, He still wrestles with what's ahead. This is the pattern Jesus gives us—and the model for how we are called to pray.

Father, if you are willing	Our request	Yet not my will but yours be done

Prayer is not just asking—it's aligning your heart to God's will. It's an act of obedience that acknowledges God's authority and opens our hearts to His greater purpose. When we pray this way, we're not only presenting our requests, but also reminding ourselves—right in the midst of our asking—that our trust is in Him.

Question:

Is your trust in God conditional? Do you trust Him more only when things seem to go your way? What should your trust be built on?

Reflections:

_____

_____

_____

_____

_____

Just Keep Knocking: Boldness, Not Hesitation

Read Luke 11:5-8.

Right after teaching the Lord's Prayer, Jesus shares a parable about a man who knocks on his friend's door at midnight asking for bread. At first, the friend resists—it's late and everyone's asleep. But the man keeps knocking, and eventually, the door opens.

Jesus isn't suggesting God is reluctant or annoyed by our petitions. He's making a contrast: if even a tired, unwilling friend eventually gets up, how much more will your heavenly Father respond to your persistence?

In Luke 18, Jesus tells a similar story—of a widow pleading with an unjust judge. The judge finally gives in, not because he cares, but because she refuses to quit. Jesus says we "ought always to pray and not lose heart" (Luke 18:1). The point is clear: keep bringing your needs to God, even when the answer seems delayed.

Hebrews 4:16 encourages us:

"Let us then with confidence draw near to the throne of grace, that we may receive mercy and find grace to help in time of need."

We come boldly—not because we deserve to be heard, but because we belong to the One who does. Yet even as we come with confidence, our motives must be in check:

"You do not have because you do not ask. You ask and do not receive, because you ask with wrong motives..." (James 4:2-3)

God invites us to approach Him—not with shallow demands or selfish desires, but with bold hearts that seek His will. We should be persistent in prayer to pursue what is truly good in His eyes.

So keep knocking. Keep asking. Ask boldly and believe that He rewards those who earnestly seek Him (Hebrews 11:6).

Suggested Prayer:

Father,

Teach me to pray with boldness and with a heart that honors You. Help me trust that You welcome my persistence, and give me the desire to seek You earnestly. Help me to ask with the right motives.

In Jesus' name,

Amen.

Question:

Have you been persistent with a particular prayer? What is your motivation for asking? Do you trust His perfect timing and plan?

Reflections:

_____

_____

_____

_____

_____

Solomon's Request: Asking According to God's Heart

Read 1 Kings 3:7-14.

When we think about asking God for something, we often default to what would make life easier—more success, more security, more comfort. But when Solomon was given the opportunity to ask for anything, he didn't go after power or safety or revenge. He asked for wisdom—a discerning heart to lead well and judge rightly.

That request shows a posture of humility. Solomon admits he doesn't know what he's doing: "I am only a little child and do not know how to carry out my duties" (v. 7). That's where prayer should begin—not with confidence in ourselves, but with a clear-eyed awareness of our need for God's wisdom.

And God responds. What mattered wasn't the eloquence of Solomon's request—it was the motive behind it. Solomon didn't ask for something to benefit himself. He asked for what would serve others and honor God. And that kind of prayer, rooted in humility and responsibility, pleased the Lord.

The story also reminds us that God knows how to bless His people. Solomon asked for wisdom, and God gave him more than he ever expected—riches, honor, and the promise of long life. It echoes the words of Jesus in Matthew 6:33: "Seek first the Kingdom of God and His righteousness, and all these things will be added to you." When we ask God for the right things—things that align with His heart—we don't have to chase everything else. He already knows what we need.

"And my God will supply every need of yours according to his riches in glory in Christ Jesus" (Philippians 4:19).

So as you come to God in prayer, don't be afraid to ask—but ask with a heart aligned to His will, trusting that He delights to give far more than we could ever imagine when our deepest desire is to honor Him.

Suggested Prayer:

Father,

Like Solomon, give me wisdom—not for my own success, but so I can live well and honor You. Help me not to chase comfort or the things the world calls valuable.

Remind me that Your Kingdom is what matters most, and that wisdom from You is better than anything else I could ask for.

In Jesus' name,

Amen.

Question:

Are there things in your life that compete for your attention? When you ask God for things, do you tend to ask more for material things, or for wisdom and discernment?

Reflections:

_____

_____

_____

_____

_____

Lesson 17

What About Fasting?

Read Ezra 8:21-23, Joel 2:12-13, and Matthew 6:16-18.

In Scripture, fasting is closely tied to dependent, heartfelt prayer. It's more than going without food—it's a posture of humility and surrender before God. In Ezra 8, God's people fasted and prayed for safe travel and protection, trusting Him more than military strength. In Joel 2, God calls His people to return to Him "with all your heart, with fasting, with weeping, and with mourning," not just with outward rituals, but with sincere repentance and a softened heart.

Jesus continued this pattern. In Matthew 6:16-18, He didn't say *if* you fast, but *when*—assuming fasting would be a regular part of a believer's life. He warned against fasting to be seen by others, teaching instead that it should be a quiet, personal act of devotion. Fasting is a way to remove distractions, slow down, and turn our full attention toward God.

Fasting also teaches us to resist the pull of immediate gratification. When Jesus was in the wilderness, He fasted for forty days before launching into His public ministry.

Read Matthew 4:1-11.

Notice how the enemy tried to undermine Jesus' identity and authority during His fast. Satan's temptations began with the words, "*If* You are the Son of God…"—a direct challenge to what God had just declared at Jesus' baptism. But Jesus didn't argue, defend Himself, or rely on physical strength. Instead, He responded every time with Scripture—anchoring Himself in truth. This was a clear moment of spiritual warfare, and Jesus met it not with power or pride, but with the Word of God.

Jesus showed us that fasting isn't just spiritual—it's about training our physical bodies and minds to know and submit to God's word.

Consider Fasting:

If you're physically able, consider setting aside one day this week to fast—not to prove something or check off a spiritual box, but to learn what it means to truly "live on" God's Word (Matthew 4:4).

Here are some ways to pray while you fast:

- Invite the Holy Spirit to speak to you and read through passages of the Bible. I recommend Romans 8 and Galatians 5.

- Ask God to create in you a hunger for His Word that's even greater than physical hunger.

- Reflect on what distractions may be pulling you away from spending time in prayer and reading God's Word.

A Personal Note

I've done a seven-day fast before, but I wouldn't recommend starting with something that intense—especially if you haven't fasted for shorter periods first. The first day, you'll likely feel hungry. The second day, you might get a headache. By the third day, your body starts to adjust, and you start to realize that your will—strengthened by God—can become stronger than your physical cravings.

For me, fasting has been a powerful way to learn self-discipline and surrender—helping me bring even my physical desires below my desire to know Him and the Scriptures more.

Disclaimer

Fasting is a personal decision, and it's not one-size-fits-all. If you're unsure whether fasting from food is right or safe for you—especially if you have medical conditions or dietary needs—please talk to your doctor first. Your health matters. Fasting should always be approached with wisdom, care, and prayer.

Prayers of Intercession

Prayer is often thought of as bringing our own needs before God, but as followers of Jesus, we're also called to intercede—to stand in the gap and pray fervently on behalf of others. Intercessory prayer is both a privilege and a vital responsibility. It reflects the heart of God and expresses our love for those around us, near and far.

From Abraham's bold bargaining for Sodom to Paul's constant prayers for the churches, Scripture is full of examples of intercession. Jesus is our perfect intercessor, praying for us continually and teaching us to do the same. This section, we'll explore what it means to pray with compassion, courage, and consistency for others.

Standing in the Gap

In Ezekiel 22:30, we find a sobering but beautiful image. God says:

"I looked for someone among them who would build up the wall and stand before me in the gap on behalf of the land so I would not have to destroy it, but I found no one."

God was looking for someone—anyone—who would be willing to stand in the spiritual space between judgment and mercy. To stand in the gap means to intercede. It's not just praying about someone, but praying for them with compassion and conviction. It means taking spiritual responsibility for others—bringing their names, their needs, and even their unspoken burdens before God.

In Ezekiel's time, no one stepped up. No one was willing to carry that burden in prayer. That's what makes this verse so weighty—it reminds us that God is still looking for people today who will take on the quiet, faithful work of intercession. It may not be visible or celebrated, but it matters deeply to the heart of God.

Often, those who stand in the gap are people who've lived through difficult things themselves.

A Personal Note

I lost my Mother in 2021 to Glioblastoma, an aggressive brain cancer. It was right at the tail end of COVID, and walking through both at once was incredibly hard. She lived for 18 months after her diagnosis. Since then, I've met others who have also lost loved ones too young, and because I've walked that road, I've been able to sit with them in their grief—and to pray. I've asked God to comfort them, to give them peace in the middle of the pain, and to remind them they're not alone.

One verse that brought me real comfort during that time was Isaiah 57:1-2:

"The righteous perish, and no one takes it to heart; the devout are taken away, and no one understands that the righteous are taken away to be spared from evil. Those who walk uprightly enter into peace; they find rest as they lie in death."

That verse helped me see my Mother's passing not just as a loss, but as a kind of mercy. Her suffering ended, and she was welcomed into peace. That truth has stayed with me.

Tragedy is never easy—but it can open our hearts to stand in the gap for others. Pain gives us perspective. It softens us, deepens us, and teaches us how to pray with compassion. Interceding for someone in the middle of their grief is a way of helping carry their burdens to the feet of Jesus.

So don't miss the chance to pray for someone walking through something hard. Your own story might be what God uses to help them find hope, healing, and the peace only He can give.

A Different Kind of Prayer List

Prayer lists often center around health concerns or immediate problems—and there's nothing wrong with that. But for this practice, I want to invite you into a different approach. Instead of starting with known needs, take a quiet moment and ask God to show you who to pray for.

You might be surprised by who comes to mind—maybe someone you haven't thought about in a long time, or someone who simply "pops into your head" for no clear reason. Many believers have shared stories of praying for someone in response to that quiet nudge, only to find out later that the person truly needed prayer in that very moment. That's the Holy Spirit at work—leading us to intercede in alignment with God's heart.

Start a prayer list—but not the way you normally would. Don't rush. Let God lead. Add names as He brings them to mind. Revisit the list over time. Sit with it, reflect on it, and faithfully intercede for the people God lays on your heart. This kind of prayer isn't reactive; it's responsive—listening first, then lifting others up as the Spirit leads.

Interceding with Courage and Compassion

Read Genesis 18:20-33.

When God reveals His plan to judge Sodom, Abraham steps forward and begins to intercede—boldly, yet humbly—asking God to spare the city for the sake of the righteous. Starting with fifty, he carefully negotiates the number down to ten, each time showing reverence, persistence, and a deep concern for others.

What's striking isn't just Abraham's boldness—it's God's response. There's no frustration or rebuke. God listens. Abraham appeals to God's justice—"Shall not the Judge of all the earth do right?" (v. 25)—but he also leans into God's mercy. His request isn't just for the righteous to be spared; it's for the whole city to be spared because of the few who still walk with God.

In this exchange, we see something profound. We see just how far God is willing to go to show mercy, even in the face of great wickedness. Though the city lacked even ten righteous people, the conversation reveals God's heart: He would have spared them. Not because they deserved it, but because mercy matters to Him.

Read Jonah 4:10-11.

After Nineveh repents and is spared, Jonah is angry—not because justice failed, but because mercy prevailed. But God challenges Jonah's narrow view with a powerful question: "And should not I pity Nineveh, that great city, in which there are more than 120,000 persons who do not know their right hand from their left...?"

This echoes the truth in 2 Peter 3:9—that God is "not willing that any should perish, but that all should come to repentance."

Let your prayers stretch beyond comfort, asking God to show mercy even to those you struggle to love. Pray with courage and pray with compassion.

Suggested Prayer:

Father,

Teach me to pray for others—for individuals, families, and entire communities in need of Your mercy. Help me also to pray for those I struggle with, and to see them through Your eyes.

Shape my heart to care about what You care about: justice, mercy, and the salvation of the lost.

In Jesus' name,

Amen.

Question:

Is there someone who comes to mind who needs prayer? Is there anyone you wouldn't normally pray for that you could lift up this week?

Reflections:

_____

_____

_____

_____

_____

Jesus: The Great Intercessor

Jesus isn't just our example in prayer—He is our intercessor. Seated at the right hand of the Father, He prays for us continually. He is our eternal, perfect High Priest who saves and intercedes for those who draw near to God. His priesthood is unchanging and anchored in His resurrected life:

"But he holds his priesthood permanently, because he continues forever. Consequently, he is able to save to the uttermost those who draw near to God through him, since he always lives to make intercession for them" (Hebrews 7:24–25).

Even before Peter denied Him, Jesus said:

"Simon, Simon, behold, Satan demanded to have you, that he might sift you like wheat, but I have prayed for you that your faith may not fail. And when you have turned again, strengthen your brothers" (Luke 22:31–32).

Jesus wasn't praying that Peter would avoid failure altogether—He was praying that Peter's faith would hold steady through it. And it did. Though Peter denied Jesus three times, Jesus restored him in love and gave him a calling: to strengthen others.

In Romans 8:34, Paul writes:

"Christ Jesus is the one who died—more than that, who was raised—who is at the right hand of God, who indeed is interceding for us."

We are not left to fend for ourselves. Even when we don't know what to pray, we're not alone:

"Likewise the Spirit helps us in our weakness. For we do not know what to pray for as we ought, but the Spirit himself intercedes for us with groanings too deep for words" (Romans 8:26).

Be encouraged—though Jesus has risen and returned to the Father, He has given us the promised Holy Spirit to help us and intercede on our behalf. Even now, your prayers are being heard!

Suggested Prayer:

Father,

Thank You that Jesus prays for me. He is always interceding, even when I don't know what to pray. Teach me to intercede for others with the same love and faith.

In Jesus' name,

Amen.

Question:

How do you feel knowing Jesus prays for you?

Reflections:

_____

_____

_____

_____

_____

Lesson 21

Paul's Pattern: A Life of Intercession

Read Ephesians 1:15-19 and Colossians 1:9-12.

Paul's letters are full of specific, heartfelt intercessions. He prays consistently—not just generic requests but for particular spiritual needs:

- That God would give spiritual wisdom and revelation.

- That believers would know the hope to which God has called them, and the riches of His glorious inheritance.

- That they would experience the greatness of His power, be strengthened, and grow in the knowledge of God.

Paul's intercession reveals his pastoral heart and his deep desire for others.

What if we prayed like that—for our churches, our friends, and even those who oppose us? How might love grow, and faith deepen, in the lives of those around us?

Pray for Three People

Commit to intentionally praying for three people every day—not casually, but with focused, persistent intercession.

- Ask the Holy Spirit to guide your prayers and intercede for you, especially when you feel unsure what to say.

- Pray boldly like Abraham—don't be afraid to approach God with compassion and courage for others.

- Pray consistently and specifically like Paul—make it a habit to pray for wisdom, strength, and growth in those you love.

Also remember to pray for your church community, that God's purposes would be fulfilled in and through your fellowship.

Suggested Prayer:

Father,

This week I desire to lift up three people You've placed on my heart:

1. _____

2. _____

3. _____

May You give them wisdom, strength, and greater faith as they look to You. I pray they would experience the greatness of Your power, be strengthened, and grow in the knowledge of You.

In Jesus' name,

Amen.

Question:

How often do you pray for the needs of others? Are your prayers similar to those of Paul? How can you pray for others differently?

Reflections:

_____

_____

_____

_____

_____

Spiritual Warfare and Praying with Authority

We live in the reality of spiritual warfare, but as followers of Jesus, we don't fight with earthly weapons. Instead, God equips us with spiritual armor and power through prayer. When our prayers are grounded in His authority and love, they break strongholds and bring light into the darkest places.

This kind of prayer requires both courage and discernment. It means standing firm in the truth of God's Word, even when circumstances push against it. It means praying not just for comfort, but for clarity, boldness, protection, and breakthrough—for ourselves and for others. Through prayer, we take our place in the battle not as spectators, but as active prayer warriors in God's redemptive work. We resist the enemy not in our own strength, but in the name and power of Jesus, who has already secured victory. This section, we will focus on spiritual warfare and praying with authority.

The Armor of God

Read Ephesians 6:10–18.

Putting on the armor of God means standing in His truth and living by it. When the enemy attacks, follow Jesus' example—speak God's Word and remember who you are in Christ. For example, holding up the Shield of Faith means saying, "God's got this. Romans 8:28 says... even if I don't understand." Read through each piece of the armor and ask God to help you put it on.

Defensive Armor

- **Belt of Truth:** Knowing and embracing God's truth steadies us amid confusion and lies. Truth holds everything together.

- **Breastplate of Righteousness:** Our standing in Christ guards our hearts against condemnation and compromise.

- **Shoes of the Gospel of Peace:** With the peace of Christ, we can stand firm even when the world is chaotic and uncertain.

- **Shield of Faith:** Faith acts as a barrier, extinguishing the fiery attacks of doubt, accusation, and fear from the enemy.

- **Helmet of Salvation:** The helmet protects our minds with the assurance of salvation, reminding us of our identity in Christ.

Offensive Weapons

- **Sword of the Spirit (God's Word):** Scripture isn't just defensive—it's our weapon. Jesus wielded it to counter Satan in the wilderness, cutting through deception and temptation.

- **Prayer:** Prayer is the power that activates the armor. Paul urges us to "pray in the Spirit on all occasions," showing that ongoing, Spirit-led prayer is our key weapon in battle.

Suggested Prayer:

Father,

Help me put on Your armor so I can stand strong in the battles I cannot see. Wrap me in truth, guard my heart with righteousness, and steady my steps with the peace of Christ. Strengthen my faith to deflect every lie and fear the enemy sends. Protect my mind with the assurance of salvation, and teach me to wield Your Word like a mighty sword.

In Jesus' name,

Amen.

Question:

Which piece of armor encourages you most? Do you only wear the armor, or do you wield the sword?

Reflections:

_____

_____

_____

_____

_____

_____

Lesson 23

The Roaring Lion: Spiritual Battles in Prayer

Read 1 Peter 5:6-10.

Do you notice any parallels to the story we read earlier in Daniel?

Just as Daniel faced real, physical lions, we face spiritual ones—anxiety, temptation, fear, jealousy. The battle we're in is no less real; it's just fought in the unseen. Daniel didn't rely on his own strength or strategy. His confidence in the lions' den came from a life grounded in prayer, where he continually reminded himself of God's power.

Sometimes God allows trials in our lives. Often, those are the very places where God does His deepest work in us—refining, strengthening, and shaping us. Jesus said, "In this world you will have tribulation. But take heart; I have overcome the world" (John 16:33).

As believers, we shouldn't be surprised by trials. In fact, we rejoice in our sufferings, knowing that suffering produces endurance, and endurance produces character, and character produces hope (Romans 5:3-4).

But not every challenge is a trial or spiritual battle. Sometimes, we're just anxious because things aren't going our way. Over the years, I've talked with many people who equated uncomfortable circumstances with spiritual warfare. But some of our battles may be self-inflicted—rooted in unconfessed sin or our refusal to surrender control. Sometimes, we're simply unwilling to step down from our own throne. We live in a fallen world, and sometimes we suffer not because of our own choices, but because of the sins of others—abuse, addiction, betrayal... there are so many things that ripple into our lives.

For the trials that are real, Peter reminds us in verse 6 that God will lift us up "at the proper time." And in verse 10: "After you have suffered a little while, the God of all grace, who has called you to His eternal glory in Christ, will Himself restore, confirm, strengthen, and establish you."

Spiritual battles often involve persecution for our faith in Christ. But they can also come in the form of accusations—subtle or direct—aimed at making us question who God says we are. If you're struggling with any of these things, you may be in a spiritual battle.

So how do we overcome?

The same way Jesus did. We pray and declare. We combat the enemy's lies with Scripture, and we remind ourselves of our true identity in Christ. We step down from the throne and declare that only God is worthy to sit there. We confess our sins and believe that He is faithful and just to forgive us and to cleanse us from all unrighteousness. We call on the power of the Holy Spirit to intercede for us, just as we've talked about throughout this book. We put on the full armor of God and stand strong in the midst of the lions.

And in all of it, we rest in the peace that comes from knowing Christ and walking in alignment with God's will.

If you're in a battle right now, there is hope. Remind yourself of the truths above, and pray for victory in Jesus' name.

Consider:

Consider watching War Room (2015), a Christian drama that highlights the power of prayer to transform lives, relationships, and spiritual priorities. If you choose to watch it, take a few moments afterward to reflect and write down your thoughts below.

Reflections:

_____

_____

_____

_____

_____

_____

Lesson 24

True Authority: Submitting to God's Will

Read 2 Corinthians 10:3–5 and James 4:7.

These passages remind us that we don't fight with worldly weapons and that we have the power to resist the devil. Notice what this spiritual power is directed toward—tearing down arguments and every lofty opinion that sets itself up against the knowledge of God. Real spiritual warfare means bringing our thoughts, desires, and agendas into obedience to Christ.

Taking our thoughts captive means we examine every idea—especially those that try to define who we are or who God is—and hold it up to the truth of Scripture. If it doesn't align, we let it go, choosing to believe God's Word over any lie. This battle is fought in the mind, and it's here that prayer becomes essential. As we take thoughts captive, we ask the Holy Spirit to help us discern truth. We pray and set our minds on things above.

Some people hear the word "authority" and assume it's something we grow into—a kind of spiritual power to perform miracles or speak with boldness. But that's a misunderstanding of what it means to have authority in Christ.

At the beginning of this book, we looked at Elijah. Remember when fire fell from heaven and consumed the altar? Even in that dramatic moment, Elijah took no credit. He said, "...and that I have done all these things at your word." His authority came from obedience, not personal power.

Test everything by the Word of God—your thoughts, your emotions, and the claims of others. Don't be swayed by confident voices or dramatic prayers, no matter how persuasive they sound. If someone claims to speak God's will over your life, don't just accept it at face value. Hold it up to Scripture, just as you would your own thoughts. Ask: Does this align with what God has already revealed in His Word? Let the Bible be your filter—not someone's passion, intensity, or charisma. And pray for discernment, so you can clearly recognize what reflects God's will and what doesn't.

Suggested Prayer:

Father,

Help me to take every thought captive. Help me begin to recognize any fear or anxiety I struggle with, and I ask You to remove those things as I trust in You. Thank You for telling me to cast all my anxieties on You because You care for me (1 Peter 5:7).

In Jesus' name,

Amen.

Question:

What do you think it means to take every thought captive to obey Christ? How can you practice that this week?

Reflections:

_____

_____

_____

_____

_____

The Power of Righteous Prayer

Read James 5:16-18.

James says, "The prayer of a righteous person has great power as it is working." He points to Elijah—"a man with a nature like ours" who prayed fervently. James isn't saying Elijah was a spiritual superhero. Elijah was an ordinary man who prayed with passion and faith. Yet, his prayers stopped the rain for over three years—and then brought it back.

What does it mean to be righteous?

For us, righteousness begins with faith in Jesus. We're declared righteous—not because of what we've done, but because of what Jesus accomplished on our behalf:

"For our sake he made him to be sin who knew no sin, so that in him we might become the righteousness of God" (2 Corinthians 5:21).

"And to the one who does not work but believes in him who justifies the ungodly, his faith is counted as righteousness" (Romans 4:5).

But righteousness isn't only about our standing before God. It also shows in how we live—repenting, obeying, and following God's will. Paul reminds us in 1 Corinthians 1:28-30 that Christ Jesus "has become for us wisdom from God—that is, our righteousness, holiness and redemption." Christ not only makes us right with God; He gives us wisdom to live according to God's purposes.

Powerful prayer flows from a right relationship with God. It means standing in His righteousness and living in obedience. Elijah's prayers were powerful because he was faithful and trusted God's plan completely.

As we've seen, powerful prayer is prayer that lines up with God's will. To understand His will, we rely on Christ, who has become our wisdom and intercedes for us. When we pray faithfully and act obediently—just like Elijah—we participate in accomplishing God's desires. That's what makes our prayers powerful.

Suggested Prayer:

Father,

Thank You that through faith in Jesus, I am made righteous and accepted by You. Help me to live each day in a way that reflects this truth. Teach me to walk in obedience and trust that Your power works through the prayers of the righteous.

In Jesus' name,

Amen.

Question:

What do you think most people believe gives prayer its power? How does that compare to what we've just studied? Why might there be differences between the two?

Reflections:

_____

_____

_____

_____

_____

_____

Listening in Prayer: Hearing God's Voice

Prayer is often thought of as speaking to God—sharing our needs, our thanks, and our desires. But prayer is equally about listening. Listening in prayer is a posture of the heart that says, "Speak, Lord, for Your servant is listening." God still speaks today—through His Word, by His Spirit, and sometimes in ways that surprise us.

At times, God's voice is overwhelming—shaking us to the core, as it did on the mountaintop with Peter, James, and John (Matthew 17:4–6). Other times, He speaks with quiet subtlety, like a whisper that can only be heard in stillness. The Holy Spirit, our Counselor, often speaks through Scripture—whether in the moment of reading or by bringing a verse to mind just when we need it most, revealing God's will with perfect timing. Whether His voice is thunderous or gentle, listening is important. We'll take a look at some examples in this section.

Lesson 26

A Gentle Whisper

Read 1 Kings 19:11-13.

The prophet Elijah experienced powerful, dramatic displays of God's presence—violent wind, a trembling earthquake, and consuming fire. Yet, God was not in any of these. Instead, Elijah heard Him in a still, small voice—a gentle whisper that came only after the noise had passed.

This moment is deeply personal. Elijah, exhausted, discouraged, and afraid, finds himself alone in a cave. It's here, in this quiet and lonely place, that God meets him.

This passage teaches us something essential about prayer and intimacy with God. While God can move in mighty, unmistakable ways, He often chooses to speak through the subtle, quiet moments when we slow down, quiet our minds, and truly listen.

Part of hearing that gentle whisper is intentionally getting away from it all. Jesus modeled this by rising early and retreating to solitary places to pray (Mark 1:35). Moses climbed Mount Sinai to meet God away from the camp's noise (Exodus 24:12). Elijah himself retreated to a cave, away from the chaos and danger (1 Kings 19:9). David often sought refuge in the wilderness to pray and seek God's face (Psalm 63:1). These moments of solitude were crucial—they created space for God's quiet voice to be heard.

We live in a world that is loud—filled with distraction, noise, urgency, and constant movement. If we're not careful, we can miss God's voice simply because we aren't still enough to listen.

Psalm 46:10 says, "Be still, and know that I am God." This isn't a passive suggestion; it's an invitation to intentional stillness.

This week, find a quiet place to get away from the noise—even if it's just a drive to a scenic overlook or a walk on your favorite trail. Bring this book along, sit down, and spend time praying. Take a moment to praise God and thank Him for all He has done and continues to do in your life. In the stillness, you may begin to hear His gentle whisper.

Suggested Prayer:

Father,

Teach me to slow down and be still. In a world full of noise and distraction, help me create space to hear Your gentle whisper. Quiet my heart, clear my mind, and draw me close so I can recognize when You speak.

In Jesus' name,

Amen.

Question:

How much of your time is spent on your phone or social media? If it's significant, consider setting aside a consistent time to be still and pray.

Reflections:

_____

_____

_____

_____

_____

_____

Lesson 27

His Sheep Hear His Voice

Read John 10:27.

Jesus said, "My sheep hear My voice, and I know them, and they follow Me."

We've talked about learning to recognize God's voice—but sometimes the issue isn't whether we *can* hear Him. It's whether we *want* to.

We live in a world that has little interest in hearing the voice of God. Many aren't seeking truth; they're seeking affirmation. Scripture warns us of this plainly in 2 Timothy 4:3: "For the time is coming when people will not endure sound teaching, but having itching ears they will accumulate for themselves teachers to suit their own passions..." That time is now. We chase voices that flatter, entertain, or reassure us that we're fine just as we are.

Our culture elevates the self—our desires, our truth, our image. We've made "self" the center. (We even have "selfies" to prove it.) But hearing God's voice requires dethroning ourselves. It means choosing His voice above our own.

When you truly want to know someone, you spend time learning who they are—not just what they can do for you. That's why reading Scripture matters. God's Word reveals His voice, His heart, and His character. If you say you love someone, wouldn't you want to know everything about them?

In John 17, Jesus prayed that we would be so close to Him that we would be "in Him," just as He is in the Father. And, as we saw in the last lesson, the Holy Spirit is the One who speaks to our hearts with a gentle whisper, always in alignment with the Father's will. Jesus promised this gift to His followers—the Holy Spirit, the third Person of the Trinity.

The Trinity can be hard to understand. One of the analogies I've used in the past comes from how digital screens work. Colors on a screen use varying percentages of red, green, and blue light. You can think of the Trinity like the red, green, and blue light—distinctly different, yet essential to create pure white light. Only when all three shine fully do we see pure white, just as Father, Son, and Spirit are always fully present, and working as one.

Jesus promised that "the Helper, the Holy Spirit, whom the Father will send in My name, will teach you all things and bring to your remembrance all that I have said to you" (John 14:26). He also said that the Spirit "will not speak on His own authority, but whatever He hears He will speak" (John 16:13). The Holy Spirit is our Helper, sent from Jesus and proceeding from the Father (John 15:26). In short, the voice of Jesus, the Holy Spirit, and God the Father are not separate—they are one, working together to guide us.

To be one of Jesus' sheep is to live in constant conversation with the Shepherd. Prayer is not just speaking—it's listening. It's recognizing His voice amid the noise of the world and responding with trust and obedience.

Through the Holy Spirit, whom Jesus promised and sent, we are able to hear Him clearly. When we quiet our hearts and tune our ears to Him, prayer becomes more than requests; it becomes relationship. And the more we know His voice, the more naturally we follow wherever He leads.

Question:

Is there someone you love so much that you instantly know their voice? How could this help you picture your relationship with God and stir a deeper desire to know Him?

Reflections:

_____

_____

_____

_____

_____

Lesson 28

Samuel's Story: A Listening Heart

Read 1 Samuel 3:1-21.

Samuel was just a boy when God called him—but he didn't recognize the voice at first. He thought it was Eli, the priest, calling him in the night. Only after Eli helped him understand did Samuel realize that God Himself was speaking.

This story reminds us of several important truths about hearing God's voice:

- God speaks to whomever He pleases—regardless of age, experience, or position. What He looks for is a heart that is open.

- Recognizing God's voice is a skill we learn over time—and often with the help of wise, spiritually mature mentors.

- Samuel's response—"Speak, Lord, for your servant is listening"—is a powerful picture of readiness. He doesn't come with conditions or demands, just a heart open to obey.

God is not distant or silent—He is near, and He desires to teach, direct, and guide us in the everyday moments of our lives. But do we recognize his voice? Do we have a heart ready to listen?

This week, I'd like you to:

- Remove distractions—silence your phone, turn off background noise, and don't think about work.

- Take 5-10 minutes during your prayer time to simply be still before God. Resist the urge to fill the silence. Just listen.

- Open your Bible and ask, "Lord, what do You want to show me?" Read slowly and attentively, listening with your heart.

Suggested Prayer:

Father,

Give me a heart like Samuel's—humble, open, and ready to listen. Teach me to recognize Your voice, even when it comes quietly or in unexpected ways. Help me lay down distractions, pride, and fear so I can respond. Speak, Lord, Your servant is listening.

In Jesus' name,

Amen.

Question:

Is there someone in your life who could mentor you in prayer? Like Eli guided Samuel, perhaps God has placed someone around you who would be willing to walk with you—someone who can help you learn to listen and recognize God's voice?

Reflections:

_____

_____

_____

_____

_____

_____

Developing A Consistent Prayer Life

A powerful and consistent prayer life doesn't just happen. It is cultivated over time—through discipline, desire, and deep intimacy with God. Jesus, more than anyone, modeled this way of life. He regularly withdrew to be alone with the Father, often before dawn or late at night. He prayed when sorrow overwhelmed Him and when purpose called Him forward. He prayed for others—and for us.

If we want to grow in prayer, we must look closely at how Jesus prayed.

Jesus intentionally rose early—before the sun—to pray alone. He didn't just squeeze prayer into His schedule as a reaction to crisis or need; He made communion with the Father His priority.

We touched on this earlier, but as we close this book, let's take a closer look…

Staying Close

Jesus made space for prayer, even when life was busy. When crowds came looking for Him, He didn't just push through. He stepped away. He found quiet places to be with the Father. The time He spent in prayer shaped everything else He did.

This was how Jesus lived—constantly connected to the Father. Prayer wasn't just a tool for hard moments. It was woven into His teaching, His healing, His decisions, even His suffering. He wasn't simply reacting to needs; He was staying in step with the One who sent Him.

He wants us to do the same—keep in step with the Spirit (Galatians 5:25). Jesus said, "Abide in me, and I in you... for apart from me you can do nothing" (John 15:4-5). This isn't about occasional check-ins—it's about living in a relationship with Jesus. Being "in Him" shapes our identity and purpose. It's where our strength, fruitfulness, and direction come from.

We've talked about alignment before, but staying close isn't just about being aligned—it's about walking in step. You can be aligned with someone but still out of step. When you're in step, your rhythm matches theirs. Your actions match theirs.

"Pray without ceasing" (1 Thessalonians 5:17) can feel overwhelming at first glance, but it points to a lifestyle, not nonstop words. It's about living with continuous communication—constant awareness of God's presence and an ongoing conversation. It's listening as much as speaking, staying tuned to God's voice throughout the day. When we do this, our lives stay aligned with God's will, and we remain in step with the Spirit.

Staying close to God is the foundation for everything else in our walk. It changes how we see the world, how we face challenges, and how we live each day. The closer we stay, the more we reflect His presence—so that others may see. That, it seems, is the whole point.

Suggested Prayer:

Father,

Help me stay close to You and walk in step with You. Teach me to trust You fully, and may I turn to You in every moment—whether life is busy or calm.

In Your name,

Amen.

Question:

It's easy to forget to pray or read the Bible. What can you do to remind yourself to stay close?

Reflections:

_____

_____

_____

_____

_____

_____

Do You Know Jesus?

If you've made it this far in the book, there's a good chance you already know Jesus and have chosen to follow Him. But I want to pause and ask—are you truly following Him? Has your faith moved beyond head knowledge into a real relationship that shapes how you live?

It's not just about believing certain things or showing up to church. It's about walking with Him daily, letting His presence shape your life. Sometimes we come to God only when we need something, or we expect blessings without really surrendering. And some resist following Jesus altogether, thinking it's just about rules. But truly knowing Him isn't about rules—it's about discovering what you were created for and learning to walk in that purpose.

When we walk closely with Him, our prayers take on new power—not because we're perfect, but because we're aligned with the One who is.

If you've never surrendered your life to Jesus, or you're unsure where you stand, you can do that right now. He's not waiting for you to clean yourself up first. He's inviting you into a relationship—just as you are.

A Prayer to Receive Jesus:

Jesus,

I know I've gone my own way, and I've sinned against You. I believe You died for me and rose again so I could be forgiven and made new. I want to walk with You. I give You my life. Come into my heart, forgive my sin, and lead me from this day forward. Jesus, I trust You as my Savior, and I want to follow You as Lord.

In Your name,

Amen.

"Just so, I tell you, there is joy before the angels of God over one sinner who repents."
Luke 15:10

Jesus Prayed for Us

Read John 17.

The night before Jesus was betrayed and arrested, He paused to pray—not only for His disciples, but for all who would believe in Him through their message. Isn't that incredible? He took time to bring others before the Father in prayer—even those who wouldn't be born for centuries. And even now, the Holy Spirit intercedes for us who believe, bringing our needs before God's throne.

In Jesus' prayer recorded in John 17, several key themes stand out:

- **Unity** — He prayed that all believers would be united, reflecting God's nature and showing the world who He is.

- **Sanctification** — He asked that His followers be set apart and changed by the truth, living differently in the world but not removed from it.

- **Protection** — Jesus prayed for our protection from the evil one, that we would have the strength and safety to faithfully carry God's name.

- **Love and Glory** — He asked that the Father's love for Him would be in us, and that one day we would be with Him to fully see His glory.

Jesus prayed for us to be united, set apart, protected, and filled with His love—so that through us, the world would come to know God. He also gave us an example of praying for others, taking the time to bring us before the Father, even as He faced what was ahead.

Read through this passage a few times. Let it sink in that the Savior of the world paused to pray for others, fully aware of the suffering He was about to endure. That alone shows how deeply He loves and cares for you.

Suggested Prayer:

Jesus,

Thank You for Your faithfulness to the Father and Your willingness to go to the cross for my sins. Help me to understand Your love for me—why You did what You did so that I could be restored and have direct fellowship with a holy God. Help me to pray for others as You did. Thank You for Your example.

In Your name,

Amen.

Question:

Following Jesus' example, who is someone you can pray for this week?

Reflections:

_____

_____

_____

_____

_____

_____

Conclusion

Becoming a Person of Prayer

Prayer is more than a discipline—it's a way of life. As we've walked through this journey together, I hope you've seen that prayer isn't just for emergencies or special occasions. It's not about performing for God, or trying to earn His attention. It's about aligning your heart with Him every day. It's about drawing near to the Father, just as Jesus did—honestly, humbly, faithfully.

We began this book with the idea of moving beyond prayer lists. Too often, we've reduced our prayer lives to a set of requests, shaped by urgency but not always by eternity. Jesus showed us a better way. He taught us to begin with the Kingdom—not our comfort. He taught us to align with God's will, not our own. And He invited us to walk in daily communion with the Father, trusting that everything else would follow in its proper place.

Through these 30 lessons, we've looked at how to:

- Pray with a Kingdom mindset

- Pray while living out our faith

- Pray with thanksgiving and worship

- Pray to confess and repent of our sin

- Pray with boldness and authority

- Pray and fast to learn to live on the Word of God

- Pray intercessory prayers, standing in the gap for others

- Pray in alignment with God's will

- Pray while listening

- Pray persistently

- Pray in the Spirit

- Pray consistently as Jesus did

If this journey through prayer has helped you grow in your faith, I hope you've taken time to reflect and write it down. And if this book has encouraged you, consider sharing it with someone who might need the same reminder: prayer isn't just a list—it's a way to align with God and join Him in accomplishing His will on earth as it is in heaven.

Keep praying.

Keep listening.

My Prayer for You

Father,

Thank You for the opportunity to write this short book. I pray it becomes a blessing to those who desire to increase their faith and draw closer to You through prayer. May their prayers be sincere—not driven by obligation, but by love. May they desire to know You more. Give them boldness as they come to recognize You more each day, and may they marvel at Your love so deeply that, in time, they will desire to share You with others.

In Jesus' name,

Amen.

www.ingramcontent.com/pod-product-compliance
Lightning Source LLC
Chambersburg PA
CBHW070334130626
46556CB00007B/2851